IT'S YOUR WORLD—CHANGE IT!
A LEADERSHIP JOURNEY

GIRLtopia™

TOWARD AN IDEAL WORLD FOR GIRLS

Girl Scouts of the USA

© 2008 by Girl Scouts of the USA

First published in 2008 by Girl Scouts of the United States of America
420 Fifth Avenue, New York, NY 10018-2798
www.girlscouts.org

ISBN: 978-0-88441-717-0

Page 20: Photo of Contemporary Arts Center by Roland Halbe.
Page 21: "Eight Slices of Pie," 2002, by Emily Martin. Ink jet on paper, aluminum and plastic pie pan. Naughty Dog Press, Iowa City, Iowa. Photo courtesy of the National Museum of Women in the Arts.
Page 25: poem by Mary Oliver from: Dream Work. © 1986 by Mary Oliver. Used by permission of Grove/Atlantic, Inc.

Independent Women, Part 1
© 2000 Sony/ATV Songs LLC, Cori Tiffani Publishing, Ekop Publishing, Sony/ATV Tunes LLC, ENot Publishing, Beyonce Publishing, New Columbia Pictures Music, Inc. All rights administered by Sony/ATV Music Publishing, 8 Music Square West, Nashville, TN 37203. All rights reserved. Used by permission.

Hammer And A Nail
Words and Music by Emily Saliers
© 1990 EMI VIRGIN SONGS, INC. and GODHAP MUSIC
All Rights Controlled and Administered by EMI VIRGIN SONGS, INC.
All Rights Reserved. International Copyright Secured. Used by Permission.

Imagine
Words and Music by John Lennon
© 1971 (Renewed 1999) LENONO.MUSIC
All Rights Controlled and Administered by EMI BLACKWOOD MUSIC INC.
All Rights Reserved. International Copyright Secured. Used by Permission.

Ethical tests, page 46, adapted from the Institute for Global Ethics® Ethical Fitness® Seminar.
© 2008 Institute for Global Ethics®. All Rights Reserved.

CONTENTS

WELCOME

TO THE JOURNE

Imagine if every girl in the world could attend school, pursue her passions, and choose the career and family life she wanted. Imagine a world in which girls could influence policies that really matter—education, health care, housing, employment.

RIGHT NOW, THIS ISN'T THE CASE. Consider these statistics:

Half the women in the world above age 15 cannot read or write. [1]

Worldwide, 62 million girls are not attending primary school. [2]

Violence causes more death and disability worldwide among women aged 15–44 than war, cancer, malaria, or traffic accidents. [3]

[1] Women's Learning Partnership/womankind.org.uk
[2] *Because I Am a Girl: The State of the World's Girls 2007* (Plan International)
[3] Directorate of Public Health, UK, via womankind.org.uk

GIRLtopia is your invitation to envision a perfect world—a utopia—for girls. On this journey, you will create an ideal community where girls' values, needs, and interests are respected and celebrated—always. And along the way, you just might discover that when you can envision a change, you can make it happen.

YOUR GUIDE
to GIRLtopia

Why GIRLtopia? explains the need for a GIRLtopia with facts, *and* invites you to create a vision of your perfect, girl-focused world through art: poetry, painting, sculpture, video—or whatever you choose.

CREATE IT gets you going with inspiration for your GIRLtopia art project.

In **DISCOVERING YOUtopia,** you'll uncover the "you" in utopia. You'll get to know your real self better than ever. And you'll explore the "ideal" you—the best you *you* can possibly be.

In **CONNECTING Toward GIRLtopia,** you'll gain strategies for partnering with others on your GIRLtopia vision. You'll build the network you need to make an *ideal world for girls.*

TAKING ACTION on Your Vision supports you as you plan, organize, and do a Take Action Project based on your vision.

Keep in mind: With this map, there's no hard and fast route to follow. So mix it up! Go forward, swing back, dip into the middle. Choose your own adventure through GIRLtopia.

What's important is that throughout this journey, you act as a *VISIONARY*—a creative thinker who can foresee a future in which girls take center stage and are empowered to make a difference in the world. That means you'll be a leader with the confidence to bring the world, locally or globally, one step closer to ideal. After all, an ideal world for *girls* really means a more ideal world for *everyone*, right?

Getting to GIRLtopia . . .
It's Up to You!
You've Got CHOICES. You Decide...

Your Level of Creativity . . .

You decide how much time to spend on your artistic vision,
how detailed to make it, and whether and how to showcase it
(see pages 20–27 for ideas).

How to Take Action . . .

GIRLtopia is crammed with information to inspire you as
you bring the world closer to your ideal. Use it to choose your
Take Action Project and to decide how to accomplish that
project—on your own or with a team. Your goal is to
use your time and resources as wisely as possible to create
the most impact.

Who's on Your Team . . .

You can take this journey with a team or solo. And your Take
Action Project, too, can be done with a team or on your own.
Either way, gathering with others from time to time to talk
and reflect can be a good thing. If you have a team, you and
your teammates will make choices together as you venture
forward. Your Girl Scout adviser will have a journey guide
with sample sessions that suggest one way to travel to
GIRLtopia—but you can partner up and customize your
journey any way you like.

But you don't have to do *all* of these things.
You can do just one, or maybe two.

On the road toward GIRLtopia, each CHOICE is yours. And you have one more CHOICE: whether or not to pursue...

THE GIRL SCOUT
SENIOR
VISIONARY
AWARD

This journey can earn you a major Girl Scout award—or not. Again, the choice is yours. To earn the Girl Scout Senior Visionary Award, here's your three-part "must-do" list:

Create It! Complete a GIRLtopia art project (in any medium, and as an individual or team effort), and then share it. (See pages 20–27 for ideas.)

Guide It! Guide others through a GIRLtopia topic: Organize a discussion, lead a meeting, or share a topic that interests you from this book—such as ethics, the Girls' Bill of Rights, or any of the various "Think About It, Talk About It" discussion subjects.

Change It! Complete the 12 stages of the Take Action process, in a team or on your own, for a big or small project that moves the world one step closer to your vision (see page 80).

REMEMBER:
THE CHOICE IS
YOURS. GET SET FOR
A GREAT JOURNEY

Why GIRLtopia?
IT'S ALL IN THE FACTS

0... number of countries in the world where women's wages equal those of men [1]

1... percentage of the world's assets held in the name of a woman [2]

2... percentage of senior management positions occupied by women in business worldwide [3]

50... percentage of sexual assaults worldwide that are against girls 15 or younger [4]

53... percentage of American 13-year-old girls who say they are unhappy with their bodies [5]

66... percentage of 15- to 19-year-olds newly infected with HIV in sub-Saharan Africa who are girls [4]

70... percentage of the 1.5 billion people living on $1 a day or less who are female [4]

75... percentage of war fatalities who are women and children [6]

100 million... number of girls missing around the world [4]

[1] Women's Learning Partnership/womankind.org.uk
[2] unesco.org, womankind.org.uk
[3] businessweek.com, womankind.org.uk
[4] *Because I Am a Girl: The State of the World's Girls 2007* (Plan International)
[5] healthyplace.com
[6] Network for Good, womankind.org.uk

UTOPIA?
Island of Ideals

The word "utopia" comes from the Renaissance author Sir Thomas More. It was the name he gave to the imaginary island of his 1516 book, *Utopia*. More's *Utopia*, a place of order and harmony, had perfect legal, political, and social systems. Residents enjoyed six-hour workdays and education for all. Plus, no one owned land, bartering took the place of money, and gemstones were simply children's toys.

Blazing Forward
About 150 years after More, Mary Cavendish wrote *A New World: The Blazing World*, the tale of a world that honored "peace before war, wit before policy, honesty before beauty."

Long Live Utopias!
The 1988 novel *The Gate to Women's Country*, by Sheri S. Tepper, depicts a future world where women spend their lives learning and rediscovering lost knowledge, free from threats of violence.

Here are some things you might wonder about as you take in all this info:

How would the world be better for everyone if we had a GIRLtopia?

What is the future for a girl who can't read?

When women don't earn enough, what happens to their children?

What issues does society categorize as "women's issues"? Why aren't they everyone's issues?

How could everyone help create a GIRLtopia?

Juliette Gordon Low

a True GIRLtopia Visionary

In 1912, Juliette Gordon Low recognized the need for a place where girls could discover their strengths as leaders, connect with other girls and adults who encourage them to succeed, and take action to better their communities.

Low believed that all girls should have the opportunity to develop physically, mentally, and spiritually. She foresaw a world in which girls were agents of change:

> **"I want to appeal to every Girl Scout,"**
> **she said, "to . . . help to make a 'newer**
> **and better world.'"**

Low's vision of a "GIRLtopia" is still going strong. Girl Scouts has grown from its original troop of 18 in Savannah, Georgia, to 3.6 million members in the United States and 90 countries around the world. And that's not counting Girl Scout alumnae—now estimated at 50 million throughout the world.

Juliette Gordon Low, right, in a French Farman plane, with aviator Laurence Driggs in 1922. The two flew over Girl Scout headquarters in New York.

In an ideal world for girls, the world will be more ideal for everyone.

think about it, talk about it

Consider the all-girl environments you know or take part in—formal ones, like Girl Scouts, and informal ones, like a group of your best girlfriends. Think about places in your own community where girls have fun together, feel empowered, and are free to be themselves.

Are there advantages to sometimes hanging out just with girls? If yes, what are they? If no, why not?

....

....

....

In an "ideal" group of girls and boys working together on a project, how do boys act?

....

....

....

How do girls relate to one another in all-girl environments?

....

....

....

Do girls sometimes change the way they relate to one another when boys are around? If yes, in a good way? In a bad way? How?

....

....

....

RATE YOUR WORLD

To make a real change in girls' lives, you need to be knowledgeable about the quality of those lives right now in the real world.

Think about your school, community, country, the world at large. What makes life hard for girls? What obstacles do girls face? Ask your friends, and check out the daily news.

Is there anything less than "GIRLtopian" in your world? How about around the globe? Who's already doing something about it?

> After the hundreds of stories I've heard of atrocities around the globe, I know that if you're a woman born in the United States, you're one of the luckiest woman in the world. take your good fortune and lift your life to its highest calling.
>
> **–Oprah Winfrey**

Look back at page 9, at one or a few of the statistics, or consider other facts that you have found. **What are your wishes for girls around the world?**

....

....

....

....

....

....

VISION = KNOWLEDGE + IMAGINATION

How would you make it real? **Brainstorm.**

....

....

....

....

....

....

imagine

\i·MA·jen\ verb: to form a mental image of (something not present)

When asked to imagine a GIRLtopia, here's what some 9th- and 10th-grade girls said:

In a perfect world,

- girls would "be strong leaders in all areas."

- girls would "be honored for their intelligence, not only their looks."

- girls would "be able to do whatever they want whenever they want, without limitations."

- girls could "choose any career or lifestyle because there would be no more stereotypes about what they can or can't do."

- girls would "feel empowered to be leaders through compassion and kindness."

S-T-R-E-T-C-H YOUR VISION

Share your wishes from page 14 with your family and friends. **What do *they* wish for?**

....

....

....

Did anyone's vision surprise you? Did you learn anything new about someone? Did someone's vision stir your own imagination?

....

....

....

In a perfect world...
girls' dreams could be limitless, and
no one would shoot them down.

15

Now, take your wishes and **BUILD** them into **YOUR VISION** of **GIRL**topia.

Complete the following phrases—and let your imagination run wild!

In an ideal world,
girls could...

....

....

girls would...

....

....

girls have...

....

....

girls are...

....

....

....

Try writing your definition of GIRLtopia.

....

....

....

....

....

visionary

\vi-zhə-NER-ē\ noun: one having unusual foresight and imagination

A visionary needs confidence and a handful of practical skills.
List *your* Top 10 qualities, values, skills, or talents for a visionary:

1. ....

2. ....

3. ....

4. ....

5. ....

6. ....

7. ....

8. ....

9. ....

10. ....

Review your list and circle those qualities, values, skills, or talents that
you have. Take a moment to appreciate them.

"Vision is the art of seeing things invisible." —Jonathan Swift, from "Thoughts on Various Subjects"

S-T-R-E-T-C-H YOUR VISION

Share your list of visionary qualities and skills with friends and family. Which do *they* think you already have?

Do they see something in you that *you* didn't even consider?

....

....

....

Which qualities, values, skills, or talents on your list do you want to develop on this journey? Write them down:

....

....

....

....

think about it, talk about it

Are all visionaries leaders? Are all leaders visionaries? Why or why not?

....

....

....

....

....

....

....

> "They say my work is just a drop in the ocean. I say the ocean is made up of drops."
>
> — Mother Teresa

GET INTERACTIVE

Get those creative juices flowing

Go Green

LISTEN IN

Anything's Possible

PAINT, WRITE, DRAW

Embrace your avatar

CREATE IT

GIRL TOPIA

There's a whole world out there to inspire you.
So take a good look.

Take it to the limit

Show it off!

Big, Small, Any Size

inspiration

\in(t)-spə-RĀ-shən\ noun: the action or power of moving the intellect or emotions

Look at some big things, like the buildings of Iraqi-born architect Zaha Hadid, where floors curve and walls twist, roofs jut and swoop, and walkways zigzag toward the sky—a great reminder that things don't have to be the way they usually are.

Look at small things, too, even pie-size—like "Eight Slices of Pie," an artist's book by Emily Martin of Iowa City, Iowa. Each slice holds a recipe and personal memories and reflections. Imagine a GIRLtopia pie in which each slice is a different size—to represent exactly what GIRLtopia needs.

Or maybe go interactive and let your viewers take part, as they do in Lygia Clark's "Cabeça Coletiva" ("Collective Head"). This mixed-media work, which the Brazilian artist created with her students, started with a wooden platform hung with food, clothing, and letters. Clark and her students took it out into the streets and let passersby take from it and add to it. Perhaps you could create a way to let viewers add to (or take away from) your GIRLtopia?

Maybe your GIRLtopia can be a haven of visual beauty and a community gathering space. In Parc Guell, a community space in Barcelona, Spain, architect Antoni Gaudí layered his

utopian vision into a fairy-tale world of light and color. Vibrant mosaic tiles decorate everything from a winding bench in a central square to a magical dragon in a stone fountain. Parc Guell was supposed to offer housing far from the city's havoc. Now it's a peaceful, public gathering place.

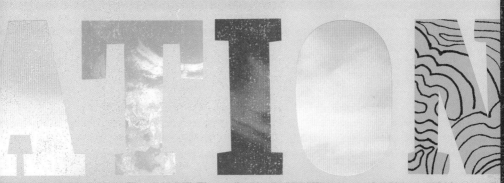

Shangri-la in *Lost Horizon,* a 1933 novel by James Hilton, is an idyllic valley hidden in the Himalayas, where the people, who never age, live in peace and harmony and abide by principles of moderation. They devote themselves to the pursuit of wisdom and enlightenment and work for the betterment of humankind. The term "Shangri-la" now often refers to any hidden paradise or dream world.

The 1937 film **"Lost Horizon"**—the big-screen version of the novel—has been called "a beautiful, feel-good movie with great performances." It's available in video and DVD. Next time you plan a movie night with friends, why not go a little retro and have a screening? See if you think Shangri-la looks like a beautiful place to live.

think about it, talk about it

Where's your Shangri-la? Where do you go to feel safe, happy, and peaceful? Is it your bedroom, a park bench, a corner of your local library, a shady spot by a creek?

Is there a place in the world you consider ideal? Or a place you imagine to be ideal that you've always wanted to visit? (Check out the travel opportunities at www.studio2b.org/escape/destinations.)

What other movies, TV shows, or songs showcase a utopia?

....

....

....

What movies, TV shows, and music speak to the world's problems and the desire for a more ideal world?

....

....

....

....

LET SONGS INSPIRE YOU

From

"Independent Women, Part 1"
by Destiny's Child

(Words and Music by Corey Rooney, Samuel Barnes,
Jean Claude Olivier, and Beyoncé Knowles)

The shoes on my feet
I've bought it
The clothes I'm wearin
I've bought it
The rock I'm rockin
I've bought it
'Cause I depend on me
If I wanted
The watch you're wearin
I'll buy it
The house I live in
I've bought it
The car I'm drivin
I've bought it
I depend on me (I depend on me)
All the women who are independent
Throw your hands up at me
All the honeys who makin money
Throw your hands up at me

From

"Hammer and a Nail"
by the Indigo Girls

(Words and Music by Emily Saliers)

But my life is more than a vision,
The sweetest part is acting
After making a decision.
I started seeing the whole
As a sum of its parts.

My life is part of the global life;
I'd found myself becoming more immobile,
When I'd think a little girl
In the world can't do anything.
A distant nation—my community,
And a street person—my responsibility,
If I have a care in the world,
I have a gift to bring.

From

"Imagine"

(Words and Music by John Lennon)

Imagine there's no countries
It isn't hard to do
Nothing to kill or die for
And no religion too
Imagine all the people
Living life in peace…

You may say I'm a dreamer
But I'm not the only one
I hope someday you'll join us
And the world will be as one

Embrace Your Avatar

Avatars are everywhere—chatrooms, discussion boards, personals pages. These graphic images, whether individual creations or characters borrowed from the worlds of superheroes and cartoons, are how real people represent themselves online.

What's your avatar? Try drawing an avatar to represent the ideal YOU in your GIRLtopia:

think about it, talk about it

One person's utopia may be another's nightmare.
Can a utopia be an ideal world for some, but not for others?
Is it realistic to expect a utopia to please everyone?
Can a truly utopian world exist?

> " Every great dream begins with a dreamer.
> Always remember, you have within you
> the strength, the patience, and the passion
> to reach for the stars to change the world. "
>
> — **Harriet Tubman**

vision

\VI-zhən\ noun: 1. a thought, concept, or object formed by the imagination
2. the act or power of imagination

> the world offers itself to your imagination,
> calls to you like the wild geese, harsh and exciting—
> over and over announcing your place
> in the family of things.
> —Mary Oliver, from the poem "Wild Geese"

You can approach your "Create It!" from any angle:

MAKE A POSTER   Build a sculpture

MAKE A DRAWING

WRITE A STORY OR A PLAY   WRITE A POEM

PAINT A PICTURE   Write a song or rap

SKETCH

CREATE A FILM OR VIDEO

visit a museum | attend a gallery opening | peruse coffee-table art books | read at a poetry slam | take some photographs | talk to an artist | draw with crayons | watch a play | design a Web page | keep a dream journal | stand on your head and see the world upside down | look at fancy pastries | pick some flowers | cut out pictures | savor a snack from another country | gaze at the stars | record children's laughter | peer through a magnifying glass | dig your hands in some clay | watch kids at play | sing in the shower

Stuck For Ideas? Try This:

Write a short poem, rap, or song that expresses your vision of **GIRLtopia**.
Include at least two of these words:

imagine   dream   respect

paradise   possible   create

VISION   lead   invent

power   justice   beauty

Or try any little way to get those creative juices flowing!

To Share Your VISION, consider these possibilities:

- Take your creation to a party.
- Explain it to younger girls.
- Display it at your Girl Scout council or local library.
- Create an online photo gallery or slide show.
- Work with others to showcase all your art projects in a gallery setting.
- Don't forget to send out invitations and publicize the unveiling of your vision.

Or come up with your own idea:

....

....

....

....

....

Imagine Your Vision on a Taxi!

More than 23,000 New York City kids and adults teamed up in fall 2007 for Garden in Transit, a first-of-its-kind art, education, and creative therapy project. Kids in schools, hospitals, and community organizations painted huge, colorful flowers onto giant decals. The decals were then placed on the hoods, trunks, and roofs of thousands of New York taxicabs. Before long, the streets were bursting with multicolored blossoms on wheels—an effort that got kids of all ages, cultures, and races to join together to beautify their concrete jungle. Can you imagine your GIRLtopia vision traveling through the world like this?

CREATE IT! Part 1 of the Visionary Award

Now that you've turned your GIRLtopia vision into art, how about a mini review?

What's your medium and why did you choose it?

....

....

What inspired you most?

....

....

What's the BIG MESSAGE you are putting forth?

....

....

What's your absolute favorite part of your CREATE IT?

....

....

What does your CREATE IT say about you? What doesn't it say?

....

....

If you could change one thing about your CREATE IT, what would it be?

....

....

If you could share your CREATE IT in more ways, how would you do so and with whom?

....

....

CREATE IT! ACCOMPLISHED

_____   _____

Signature   Date

Ethical you

Decisions decisions

Who is it you want to be?

Discovering YOUtopia

GIRL TOPIA ™

Who are you now?

Who is the person you aspire to be?

VALUES

NAME YOUR

Feeling confident?

Lead on!

Got courage

Make your day!

leader

\LĒ-dər\ noun: a person who has commanding authority or influence

In Girl Scouts, girls become leaders from the inside out by:

Discovering themselves and their values

Connecting with others, and

Taking Action to improve the world.

Imagine you are the leader of your own ideal world. What kind of leader would you be? What makes a good leader? What makes an ideal leader?

What's on Your List? Name your Top 10 leadership qualities (values, skills, or talents):

1. ....

2. ....

3. ....

4. ....

5. ....

6. ....

7. ....

8. ....

9. ....

10. ....

Review the list you've just created. Which qualities or skills do you already have? Are there any qualities or skills on the list that you want to develop on this journey? What can you do to develop them?

....

....

Ask friends, family, or others in your world to make their own list of leadership qualities. Compare their lists to yours. What's the same? What's different? What did you learn about them?

think about it, talk about it

Leaders are wide-ranging, from presidents and corporate executives to community activists or artists to personal role models to someone who does a small act that makes a difference. Think about situations in your own life where you used your various leadership skills.

What's YOUR leadership philosophy?

Write it down.

LEADER

put your definition here:

Leadership Bracelet

Make one for yourself or someone you admire. Using your "Top 10 Leadership Qualities" list, assign each quality a color bead. (Red might represent courage; yellow, a sunny outlook on life.) Then, string the corresponding beads into a symbolic bracelet.

Ode to a Leader

Write a letter of appreciation to a woman you consider a role model. Choose someone you know personally or a widely known leader. Consider including one of the following phrases: "You inspire me because . . . " or "One way in which I imagine I am like you is . . . " Present, or send, your letter to your role model.

Leadership Talk Show

Create a "talk show" (for radio or TV) that features interviews of top female leaders. Make a list of women who have made a difference in the world, internationally, nationally, locally, or personally. Brainstorm questions to ask them. Arrange chairs for the host and "guests" (girls pretending to be those women leaders). Take turns being the interviewer. Consider turning your show into a public performance.

think about it, talk about it

● When you were being interviewed, what message did you want to get across?

● What did it feel like to be the leader?

● Did you speak differently from the way you usually do? How? Why?

● Do you think a group of boys or men would have a different discussion? Why or why not?

Fine-Tune Your Vision

• Are there any real-life leaders you'd like as role models in your ideal world? if yes, who are they and why did you choose them?

....

....

• How about leaders who, in your opinion, misuse or abuse power? What would you say to them, and what role would they play in your world?

....

....

courage

\KəR·ij\ noun: the quality of mind or spirit that enables one to face danger, fear, or difficulty with bravery

To create a better world, you need the courage to speak up for yourself and others.

> **Every time you show your courage, it grows.**
> —Juliette Gordon Low

Got Voice?

Think of all the communities you feel a part of. Where do you feel your voice is heard?

	AT HOME	AT SCHOOL	AT.........	AT..........
I FEEL COMFORTABLE EXPRESSING MYSELF	YES NO	YES NO	YES NO	YES NO
I FEEL COMFORTABLE STATING MY POINT OF VIEW	YES NO	YES NO	YES NO	YES NO
I FEEL THAT MY OPINION MATTERS	YES NO	YES NO	YES NO	YES NO
I FEEL COMFORTABLE DISAGREEING	YES NO	YES NO	YES NO	YES NO

think about it, talk about it

In your community, does anything prevent you from expressing yourself? If yes, what? What can you do about those obstacles?

at home

at school

at ....

at ....

Think about how you communicate. Are you passive, aggressive, or assertive? Is your communication style effective in getting your voice heard?

- Being passive is not expressing your feelings, hiding behind silence (it heightens hostility).
- Being aggressive is expressing yourself in a threatening, sarcastic, or humiliating way (it triggers hostility and can lead to conflict).
- Being assertive is asking for what you want or saying how you feel in an honest and respectful way that does not infringe on another's safety, dignity, or well-being (it engenders respect).

Check out the strategies for being heard on the next page.

Get Voice!

Give yourself a voice makeover. Check out the strategies below for being heard:

- **Be a good listener:** Ask good questions; listen nonjudgmentally; paraphrase what the other person is saying; show empathy for the other person's position.
- **Express your feelings** with phrases such as "I think," "I feel," or "I believe" (instead of bursting out with raw emotion).
- **Use assertive communication:** Say what you think and feel in an honest and respectful way that does not infringe on another's safety, dignity, or well-being.
- **Identify passive and/or aggressive communication in others:** "I think you are not telling me how you really feel," or "I feel that I can't talk with you when you speak in a threatening or sarcastic way."

Just for fun

With a friend, act out the original conversation and the new scenario you write for the chart on page 37. Discuss the different outcomes.

In an ideal world, everyone's voice would be equally valued.

Leaders care that all voices are heard.

FOR THE RECORD

Keep a journal about your voice makeover. Celebrate successes. Reflect on more effective ways to make your voice heard.

Write a scenario to optimize your voice—and improve your communications.

YOUR REAL-LIFE SITUATION	LAST CONVERSATION	NEW SCENARIO
....	He/She said:	He/She said:
....	....	....
....	You said:	You said:
....	....	....
....	He/She said:	He/She said:
....	....	....
....	You said:	You said:
....	....	....
....	OUTCOME:	NEW OUTCOME:
....	....	....
....	Modes of communication used:	Modes of communication used:
....	....	....

think about it, talk about it

Think of a leader you admire. How does she make her voice heard?

confidence

\KAN-fə-dən(t)s\ noun: belief in oneself and one's powers or abilities

Leaders have confidence in their abilities, and they seek opportunities to expand their knowledge and skills. So discover your skills (which you'll use to plan and carry out your Take Action Project). Fill in or check off as much as you can:

MY ACTIVITIES/CLUBS:
Example: Girl Scout cookie sales

SKILLS/TALENTS THEY REQUIRE
Making a sales pitch, keeping track of inventory

....

....

....

MY JOBS/INTERNSHIPS:
Example: babysitting

SKILLS/TALENTS THEY REQUIRE:
Creating fliers, nurturing, inventing games

....

....

....

ARE YOU:

- ○ outgoing?
- ○ an idea person?
- ○ a conflict mediator?
- ○ a writer?

- ○ a logical thinker?
- ○ a people person?
- ○ patient?
- ○ impulsive?

- ○ a problem-solver?
- ○ good with numbers?
- ○ good at public speaking?
- ○ an athlete or dancer?

DO YOU:

- ○ have musical talents?
- ○ have artistic talents?

- ○ work well with kids?
- ○ like techy stuff?

- ○ follow through on plans?
- ○ think like a scientist?

TAKING ACTION WITH CONFIDENCE

Elizabeth, 18, used her computer skills to build a Web site for Good Shepherd Services of Orlando, a grassroots program for homeless women and children in Florida. Elizabeth taught the staff how to maintain the site, and within a week, the organization had greatly broadened its clientele. Thanks to the powerful reach of the Internet, this Florida-based group was soon helping people from as far away as Ohio!

HELPING THE WORLD RIGHT FROM HOME

When 15-year-old Neela visited her grandmother in India, she was horrified by the many gaunt and ragged beggars and children living on the streets. Back home in Texas, Neela decided to use her science smarts to fight world hunger. She tested various concentrations of vitamin B nutrients to see which would be best for cloning potatoes. She discovered that a full-strength vitamin mix was best for the plants, but a less costly half-strength solution produced fine results. Her experiments won her the 2005 Discovery Channel Young Scientist Challenge and the title of "America's Top Young Scientist."

character

\KER-ik-tər\ noun: 1. moral excellence and firmness 2. reputation

Character is how you act and what you do every day. Are you honest when it's tempting not to be? Do you speak up when it's important? The "ideal you" can feel proud of your character and the things you do and say.

S-T-R-E-T-C-H YOUR VISION

Share stories about the "good acts of character" you and others have done. Find a quiet place for talking and take turns telling stories. Use lots of details—who, what, when, where, why, and how. Tell a story about:

- Being honest in a tough spot

- Going the extra mile to help someone

- Respecting oneself (Hint: perhaps by not giving in to peer pressure)

- Respectfully disagreeing with another person

- Showing courage by standing up for someone else

- Taking responsibility when no one else will

- Using resources fairly

- Doing something to make the world a better place

think about it, talk about it

What do you think is the relationship between character and leadership? Do you think developing a strong and good character is an important leadership skill? Why or why not? Consider leaders you know—personally, in your community, nationally, and globally.

Character and Leadership

CHARACTER	A LEADER WHO HAS THIS QUALITY
HONESTY	
Integrity	
HUMILITY	
Responsibility	
Effort	
Pride	

ethics

\E-thiks\ noun: a set of moral principles or values

Ethics is the subject of dealing with what is right and wrong, and what moral obligation we have to behave in a right way. Ethics is a code of values to guide our choices and our actions, and the course of our lives.

Ethics in your own life, or doing the right thing

Sometimes it's easy to tell right from wrong.

Would you:

- ◯ Steal from your friend?
- ◯ Cheat on a test?
- ◯ Spray graffiti on a building?
- ◯ Download music illegally from the Internet?

Other times it's a little more complicated.

Would you:

- ◯ Buy your favorite brand of clothes after you learn that the company uses child labor?
- ◯ Tell friend A's secret to friend B when friend A steals your boyfriend?
- ◯ Keep a ring that you tried on at a store after accidentally going all the way home while still wearing it?

What other girls say

A survey by Girl Scouts of the USA, "The Beliefs and Moral Values of America's Children," presented high school students with hypothetical situations that required moral decisions.

5% of the students would take money from their parents without asking

36% of the students would lie to protect a friend who vandalized school property

66% of the students would cheat on an exam

How would your friends respond? Ask them to take the "Ethics in Your Own Life" quiz on the previous page and compare answers.

think about it, talk about it

Do leaders have a special responsibility to make good ethical decisions? Why or why not?

To whom would you go for advice when trying to make a difficult decision? Which adults would you turn to? Which friends?

FIGURING OUT YOUR ETHICAL STANDARDS

What are your ethical standards based on? Check all that apply:

- ☐ Whatever does the most good and the least harm
- ☐ Whatever treats everyone as fairly and equally as possible
- ☐ Whatever is best for most people in the community
- ☐ Whatever is consistent with your character

Although not everyone shares the same sense of personal ethics, most people in the world have many ethical principles in common. Think of the Golden Rule! It can be found in various forms around the world—and throughout the centuries:

Confucianism
What you don't want done to yourself, don't do to others.

Buddhism
Hurt not others with that which pains thyself.

Jainism
In happiness and suffering, in joy and grief, we should regard all creatures as we regard our own self, and should therefore refrain inflicting on others such injury as would appear undesirable to us if inflicted upon ourselves.

Hinduism
Do naught to others which if done to thee would cause thee pain.

Christianity
So in everything, do to others what you would have them do to you, for this sums up the Law and the Prophets.

Zoroastrianism
Do not do unto others all that which is not well for oneself.

Sikhism
Treat others as thou wouldst be treated thyself.

Judaism
What is hateful to you, do not do to your neighbor.

Islam
Hurt no one so that no one may hurt you.

Do you know any other versions?

RIGHT VS. WRONG: KNOWING THE DIFFERENCE

Answering no to most of the questions in the following four tests will probably leave no doubt in your mind that an action is wrong.

LEGAL Test: Is this choice against the law? You can break the law by mistake, but you can also choose to break it. Do you know the consequences?

GUT-FEELING Test: What's your gut feeling? Physical reactions often let us know we might need to think a bit more before taking action.

TOP-NEWS-STORY Test: Would you feel proud of your choice if it were the day's top news? What would your friends, parents, or community think?

ROLE-MODEL Test: Think of a person you highly respect, perhaps a leader you know, and ask yourself if she would make the same decision you are considering.

ALSO, APPLY THESE THREE LENSES:

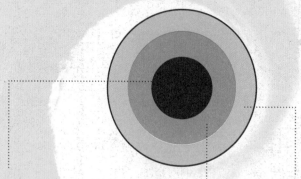

PERSONAL
When faced with making an ethical decision, consider the four tests above and think of situations in your life when one or more of the tests applied.

LOCAL
Scan the local news and consider what kinds of ethical dilemmas your community faces. Ask others what kinds of ethical issues they think your community faces.

GLOBAL
What kinds of ethical decisions do you face as a global citizen? Consider ethical issues that concern everyone—environmental, economic, social, technological, political.

Be an Ethics Coach

Use your ethical standards to advise the girls in the following scenarios. Try to incorporate the Legal, Gut-Feeling, Top-News-Story, and Role-Model tests.

Victoria and two friends are at the multiplex, deciding which movie to see. No one agrees. "Why don't we buy tickets to 'Rocket Girl,' which starts now, and then we can just slip into the theaters that are showing the other movies afterward," Kayla suggests.

"I don't think it's right to see three movies if we only pay for one," Erin says. "I'm buying a ticket to 'Emma's Diary' for later this afternoon. You two can do whatever you want."

Victoria can only pay for one ticket.

How would you advise Victoria to do the right thing?

....

....

....

....

....

Mandy was having a great time dancing and singing karaoke at Kanchana's party. When she went upstairs to use the bathroom, she accidentally walked into Kanchana's bedroom, where she found her best friend, Olivia, looking through Kanchana's jewelry.

Olivia picked up a silver-and-turquoise bracelet and put it on her wrist. "I'm just going to wear this on my date tomorrow—it matches my outfit," Olivia said. "Don't tell Kanchana—I'll put it back when we come here for our Girl Scout meeting next week."

Mandy was pretty sure Olivia would return the bracelet undamaged, but was it still OK for her to borrow it without asking?

How would you advise Mandy to do the right thing?

....

....

....

Kendra skipped a Sunday outing with her friends to Amazing Adventures Amusement Park so she could study for a World History test. When she took the test Monday morning, she felt really good about her answers. When she stopped at her locker to get her lunch, Zach, a hottie who had been on the Amazing Adventures trip, stopped her.

"Hey, Kendra, I have World History last period. Can you tell me what the test questions are?" he asked, winking.

Kendra has a huge crush on Zach. It would be so easy to rattle off several of the exact questions she remembered from the test.

How would you advise Kendra to do the right thing?

....

....

....

Paola spotted her teammates from field hockey standing near the bonfire, holding marshmallows over the flames. "Yum—S'mores," she thought as she wove through the crowd of teens gathered on the beach for an end-of-summer bash.

When she reached the S'mores makers, Imani, the hockey team goalie, handed her a stick and a bag of marshmallows. Another girl gave her a red plastic cup with some golden, frothy liquid in it—beer.

When Paola lived in Spain, she had been allowed to drink a glass of wine with dinner sometimes, but alcohol is illegal for teens in the United States.

How would you advise Paola to do the right thing?

....

....

....

Tasneem was at the grocery store to buy some apples that were on sale for just 50 cents a pound. She wanted to try out a recipe for her aunt's caramel-pecan apple pie.

As she was picking out her apples, Lucas, a classmate from school, walked up to her. "You should really buy organic apples from the farmers' market across the street. Not only are they free of pesticides, you would be supporting local farmers!"

Tasneem feels torn between wanting to save money and supporting local organic farming.

How would you advise Tasneem?

....

....

....

Watch
the 2002 movie
"John Q."

John Q. Archibald, played by Denzel Washington, is an unemployed factory worker in this PG-13 film. When his young son needs an emergency heart transplant, the hospital administrator claims that John's insurance won't cover the procedure because it's too expensive. Knowing his son will die without the transplant, John holds the hospital emergency room hostage in a desperate attempt to save the boy's life.

think about it, talk about it

Is it OK to commit a crime to save the life of a child?

yes   no

Would it make a difference if:
. . . you would be saving a 45-year-old instead?

yes   no

. . . the 45-year-old was your dad?

yes   no

. . . another child/person will die if you save this one?

yes   no

The Promise and Law
Official Girl Scout Values

The Girl Scout Promise and Law are shared by every member of Girl Scouting. Since Juliette Low founded the Girls Scouts in 1912, more than 50 million girls have pledged to live by these values. Read the Girl Scout Promise and Law below. Reflect on what they mean to you.

In addition to belonging to Girl Scouts, you belong to YOU. What's your promise and law? Choose the line from the Promise or Law that means the most to you. Use it to start or end your own Promise and Law.

....

....

....

The Girl Scout Promise

On my honor, I will try:
    To serve God* and my country,
    To help people at all times,
    And to live by the Girl Scout Law.

The Girl Scout Law

I will do my best to be
    honest and fair,
    friendly and helpful,
    considerate and caring,
    courageous and strong, and
    responsible for what I say and do,
and to
    respect myself and others,
    respect authority,
    use resources wisely,
    make the world a better place, and
    be a sister to every Girl Scout.

* Girl Scouts of the USA makes no attempt to define or interpret the word "God" in the Girl Scout Promise. It looks to individual members to establish for themselves the nature of their spiritual beliefs. When making the Girl Scout Promise, individuals may substitute wording appropriate to their own spiritual beliefs for the word "God."

A team of Girl Scouts

You and your friends?

GOOD NEIGHBORS

belong

together

CONNECTing Toward

Multiple perspectives

with

Who's with you?

team up!

GIRL TOPIA
™

ceremony

You and me

Other voices

COLLABORATE Virtual club?

Our rights

GUIDE IT! Part 2 of the Visionary Award

Choose a GIRLtopia topic that really gets you thinking and then inspire others to be visionaries! Challenge them to develop their own visions. Or motivate them to research community issues. Or teach about teamwork. Or maybe show them how to market an idea or think through an ethical decision.

1. What's your topic? _____

If you're on this journey with others, you can lead a session for them. If not, you can **share something you learned** by:

- organizing a discussion with your friends
- leading a club meeting
- creating a workshop for younger girls
- facilitating an activity for a school group
- other: _____

2. Who is your audience? _____

3. How much time will you need? _____

4. When will you do it? _____

5. Will you need to publicize? _____

Tips

- Get help (from a family member, friend, teacher, or adviser).
- Invite an expert to help (local leader, foundation board member, college professor).
- Have the meeting somewhere that's related to your topic (museum, bookstore, courthouse).

GUIDE IT! ACCOMPLISHED

— — — — — — — — — — — — — — — — — —

Signature   Date

rights

\rīts\ noun: things that are due to people by law, tradition, or nature

> " We hold these truths to be self-evident, that all men and women are created equal; that they are endowed by their Creator with certain inalienable rights; that among these are life, liberty, and the pursuit of happiness. "
>
> —Declaration of Sentiments, Seneca Falls, N.Y., 1848

The Preamble of the Declaration of Independence of 1776 declared it self-evident that all MEN are created equal. Women's rights activists Elizabeth Cady Stanton and Lucretia Mott took the idea one step further. In the Preamble to their Declaration of Sentiments, written for the first Women's Rights Convention in 1848, they declared it "self-evident" that " all MEN AND WOMEN are created equal." At that time, women had few rights: They could not vote, husbands had legal power over their wives, most professions were closed to women, and women were denied access to higher education.

A lot has changed since then, because a lot of women took action to change the world.

In 1869, Elizabeth Cady Stanton and Susan B. Anthony formed the National Woman Suffrage Association to fight for women's right to vote. They worked with other suffragists and abolitionists. They believed an ideal world would be one in which the voices of women of all races were heard, respected, and valued.

Look back at page 9 and all the statistics about the state of the world for girls. Then decide how best to spell out the rights that all girls need.

Global Girls' Bill of Rights

Preamble/Statement of Purpose

We feel it is necessary to uphold girls' rights because:

....

....

....

We declare these rights to be self-evident, that all girls:

1. ....

2. ....

3. ....

4. ....

5. ....

6. ....

7. ....

8. ....

think about it, talk about it

To what length would you go to stand up for your rights?

....

....

....

Who or what might stand in your way?

....

....

....

How could you stand up for girls' rights in your circle of friends, school, family, community?

....

....

....

Does passing a law ensure that individuals' rights will be secured? Why or why not?

....

....

....

" We've chosen the path to equality,
don't let them turn us around."

—Geraldine Ferraro, first woman nominated
to run for vice president of the United States

ceremony

\SER-ə-mō-nē\ noun: a formal act or set of acts prescribed by ritual or custom

A ceremony celebrates a special happening or honors an important occasion by expressing respect, praise, gratitude, happiness, or sorrow. A sense of oneness can come from sharing a ceremony. A ceremony at the start of a Girl Scout session offers a moment to celebrate your time together and separate it from the rest of the day. A ceremony at the end of a meeting can honor the meaningful time spent together. Ceremonies may be borrowed from tradition; new ceremonies can become tradition.

Remember: Ceremonies are not a "must-do"; they're part of the fun of being a Girl Scout. They can be simple and short, created to suit the mood of the hour, place, or occasion. Carry them out in a spontaneous and dignified manner. Consider including:

MEMORIZED LINES

SONGS

circle

CHANT

spontaneous remarks

A FEW CEREMONY SUGGESTIONS FROM TEEN GIRL SCOUTS

Smudge, from Gabby, 19: "One girl lights a smudging stick or incense at the start of the meeting, and while she walks around the room with it, another girl says, 'We make this a safe and supportive place of positive energy and belonging.'"

Spoken Word, from Anjali, 15: "In my Girl Scout troop, we always end each meeting with everyone standing and shouting at the same time, 'We have the power to change the world.'"

Hope Circle, from Dara, 16: "Everyone holds hands in a circle, and each girl says something about what she hopes will happen at the meeting or in the week ahead."

Start with a Tea Ceremony

In a proper Japanese tea ceremony, the guest and host are in harmony with each other and the universe. Start a session with your own version of a tea ceremony. Invite each participant to sip tea in silence and strive for stillness. Let each person in the room enjoy her tea and a few moments of quiet reflection on how she can bring peace and harmony to the meeting.

What would be an ideal ceremony in your GIRLtopia?

belonging

\bē-LONG-ing\ noun: feeling accepted as a member of a group

In a GIRLtopia, all girls would feel that they belong and are a valued part of the group. Take a moment to think of all the communities in which you have that same feeling of belonging.

PLACES I BELONG (MY COMMUNITIES)

In each square, put the name of a community to which you belong (Girl Scouts, family, neighborhood, world). Then record your answers to the following questions:

- Do you feel you are a valued member of this community? Why or why not?
- Do you feel supported by this community? Why or why not?
- Would you change anything in this community to make it more ideal?
- What quality, talent, or skill can you offer to make this community a better place?

REUNITING KIDS WITH THEIR CULTURE

Concerned about how lack of exposure to cultural roots has a long-term effect on children, Minna, 16, of Minnesota, created "Reuniting China with Her Children," a program that helps familiarize adopted kids born in China with the Chinese language and culture. For more than five months, Minna held classes for various age levels at a community church. She received her Girl Scout Gold Award for this project.

LETTING TEENS REALLY BELONG

In Wisconsin, Sarrah, 17, created a forum where Muslim teens could explore and embrace their identity. Through panel discussions, they could talk about religious, social, and cultural issues in a supportive environment.

think about it, talk about it

How can you make sure GIRLtopia is a place where others feel they belong? Ask your parents, friends, and teachers what makes them feel valued in a group. List the criteria that most people agree on:

....

....

cooperation

\kō-ä-pə-RĀ-sh n\ noun: working or acting together for a common purpose or benefit.

Leaders recognize the value of teamwork. This means examining ideas from a variety of viewpoints, and constructively preventing or resolving conflicts. Making group decisions can be difficult, so here are some tips to guide group decision-making:

- Present the issue in a clear way.
- Look for solutions everyone can agree on.
- Make sure each voice is heard and each opinion is valued.
- If people stray off topic, gently guide them back to the subject at hand.
- Summarize the arguments, pro and con. Take notes (or invite someone to) on a large sheet of paper that everyone can see.
- Brainstorm solutions. Synthesize points of view; jot down ideas.
- Seek consensus. Ask: Can we all agree on this? If not, seek compromise. Each side may need to make concessions. Voting is another way to arrive at a group decision. Just be sure the ideas of the minority are heard and incorporated.
- Record the decision. Include some notes about the decision-making process. Keep these notes as guidelines for group members as they move forward with their projects.

think about it, talk about it

How would people in your ideal world make decisions? What is the role of a leader in facilitating group decisions?

....

....

....

....

teamwork

\TĒM-wərk'\ noun: cooperative or coordinated effort in the interests of a common cause

Leaders build effective teams by holding themselves and their team members accountable for their work toward shared goals. What skills or talents will you contribute? Remember: Other people are counting on you to do your part!

Check off the tasks/roles that you would like to take on as part of a team. Then sign the pledge to fulfill those tasks.

visual arts

- ⭕ photography
- ⭕ video
- ⭕ drawing
- ⭕ painting
- ⭕ collage
- ⭕ sculpture
- ⭕ ceramics
- ⭕ metalwork

entrepreneurial

- ⭕ sales
- ⭕ marketing
- ⭕ publicity
- ⭕ customer relations

theater / dance

- ⭕ playwright
- ⭕ actor
- ⭕ director
- ⭕ choreographer
- ⭕ dancer
- ⭕ stage/set design

music

- ⭕ songwriting
- ⭕ singing
- ⭕ playing musical instrument
- ⭕ band member
- ⭕ deejay
- ⭕ rapper
- ⭕ music editing
- ⭕ CD maker

publications (print or online)

- ⭕ reporter/writer/poet
- ⭕ researcher
- ⭕ fact checker
- ⭕ editor
- ⭕ layout designer
- ⭕ illustrator/graphic artist
- ⭕ Web designer
- ⭕ proofreader
- ⭕ delivery/distributor

people skills

- ⭕ public speaking
- ⭕ telephoning
- ⭕ interacting with diverse people
- ⭕ conflict-resolving
- ⭕ problem-solving

Fill in the space below with the tasks you choose.
Then sign the pledge to fulfill your responsibilities.

What are you going to do?

I pledge to fulfill these tasks/roles in a timely fashion
to the best of my ability.

Signature   Date

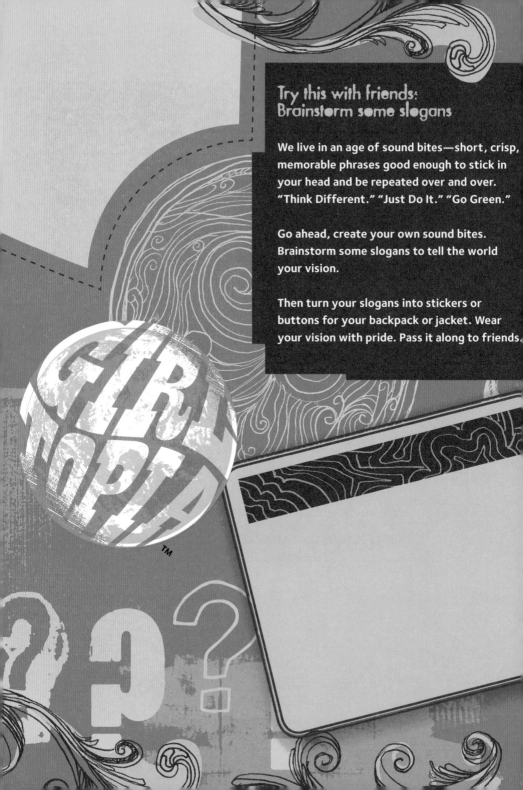

Try this with friends:
Brainstorm some slogans

We live in an age of sound bites—short, crisp, memorable phrases good enough to stick in your head and be repeated over and over. "Think Different." "Just Do It." "Go Green."

Go ahead, create your own sound bites. Brainstorm some slogans to tell the world your vision.

Then turn your slogans into stickers or buttons for your backpack or jacket. Wear your vision with pride. Pass it along to friends.

GIRLTOPIA™

networking

\NET-wərk-ing\ noun: the exchange of information or services among individuals, groups, or institutions

Who's in YOUR network?

When you hear the word "networking," you might think of online social networking—sites where you can stay connected, reinforce existing friendships, or make new connections.

Community networking goes a step further. It connects people with a shared goal or purpose—making a difference. You can build your network to include other girls in your council as well as individuals in your community. By creating a network for your Take Action Project, you build excitement and momentum for your cause. You may create some meaningful new relationships, too.

Where to start?

Your community networking will be most successful if you begin with people and organizations that:

care about your issue or have shown a commitment to similar issues

have the skills you need

have the services or resources you need

Use the community mapping section on pages 91–93 to **identify** people and organizations that can support your effort.

Once you identify them, **reach out** to them. Articulate your vision: What is your goal? What will you work together to change? Know your members: What are the needs and goals of each stakeholder? What strengths and skills do they contribute?

Don't Forget **the 'Net.** You can network in cyberspace as well. With parental permission, locate (or set up) "gathering places" (chat rooms, discussion forums, mailing lists) to share ideas about, and gain support for, your effort. You'll likely discover some useful tips for finding the right people for your network.

Turn Your Network into **NetPLAY.** Get your friends involved. Share new and interesting experiences and, as a team, join forces to make your community better—for all girls!

"The youth of the world should have standards and ideals in common."

—Juliette Gordon Low

activate

All together now!

My city

Who can help?

My neighborhood

tools

My planet

SUCCESS

MAKE A DIFFERENCE

plan

TAKING ACTION

GIRL TOPIA™

power to create

global

on Your Vision

A visionary dreams, but also TAKES ACTION to make real change. Your Take Action Project can bring the world one step closer to GIRLtopia.

EXECUTE

MAKE YOUR VISION REAL
TAKE ACTION

As you decide how to move the world a little (or a lot) closer to GIRLtopia, keep in mind that your actions will likely fall into one of two basic categories: direct and immediate action or longer-lasting efforts.

Direct and immediate *service* changes something right now.
Here are some examples:

- Organizing a book drive to help nonnative speakers of English improve their reading skills
- Setting up a career fair for women in your area
- Holding a "Take Back the Night" march

Longer-lasting *action* gets at the root of issues.
Here are some examples:

- Organizing an ongoing after-school reading assistance project
- Teaching older women computer skills so they can better compete in the job market
- Working with the town to create monthly "Teen Nights," so everyone can have fun in a safe, inclusive, and respectful environment

SERVICE VS. ACTION: WHAT'S THE DIFFERENCE?

Being of service to others means being helpful—doing the right and kind thing. Serving is often the immediate, and much needed, response to tragedy. But service is also an everyday kindness. We are of service when we feed the hungry, offer clothing to the homeless, or simply help a friend with a tough homework assignment. In serving, we are most mindful of basic human needs: food, clothing, shelter, care. **Being of service is a vital way to help and care.**

When we move beyond immediate and necessary service to understand the root causes of a problem, we move toward action. When we team up and mobilize others in our efforts to find ways to solve that problem, we are taking action. Action can happen in many ways— from partnering with your town or school to organize more sports events for girls to getting the local toy store to stop following stereotypes when selecting its inventory of merchandise for girls to holding "Take Back the Night" events so teens have a safe and fun place to hang out together once a month.

Service makes the world better for some people "right now." Action strives to make the world better for more people for a much longer time. Sometimes, service and action just naturally blend together into one sustainable effort. As a Girl Scout, you use both service and action to live out the Girl Scout Law and "make the world a better place."

Sustainability: Reach for It!

To strive toward lasting change, think about how projects can become a way of life and continue over a long period of time. In other words, consider sustainability. For example, if you are concerned about violence against girls and women, you could do any of the following:

- Organize one after-school self-defense class (direct and immediate action).
- Post fliers in your neighborhood with the phone number of a domestic violence hotline (direct and immediate action).

To create even longer-lasting change, you could:

- Get your school to offer a self-defense class every semester, for every girl (even bigger: get the whole school district to do it!).
- Plan and establish a safe place in your community where girls and women can receive support and resources.

No matter how you Take Action, your efforts are likely to raise **awareness** about your issue—and that in itself will attract more people to your cause.

SUCCESSFUL PLANNING = SUCCESSFUL PROJECTS

From small actions to large-scale community projects, you can have a significant impact on your world, locally and globally. Strategy expert Willie Peterson says, **"Strategy is the best use of scarce resources."** So before committing to an action, assess your time and resources (the time you can commit and the number of people who will help you).

Although you always want to strive toward sustainability, creating a sustainable project is not a GIRLtopia requirement (or necessary for earning the Visionary Award). Consider a strategy that will aim for sustainability and big impact by thinking about where your project falls on the continuum toward lasting change. Remember: A small, well-thought-out action using your time, resources (like your network), and brain power can have more impact than a "larger" but less focused effort. And sometimes you can create ways to Take Action that fit right in with the rest of your life—maybe even into your school day. Check it out.

1. The Case of the Goody Bags

Tamara, Gayle, and Leticia read a news story about women and children in a local shelter for battered women. These families often left their homes with almost nothing, in order to escape physical abuse. Wanting so badly to help even though they were really busy, the three friends jumped into action. They made posters to rally other kids at school to bring in small toys, stickers, and art supplies for the children at the shelter. Within no time, the girls had created 45 goody bags bulging with fun stuff. Gayle called the shelter and arranged to stop by and meet with the social worker.

When the three friends arrived at the shelter, instead of 45 children, the girls counted only 10 kids between the ages of 2 and 5. They were all playing happily in a colorful room well stocked with games. The social worker explained that a wealthy private donor kept the shelter supplied with toys, games, books, and clothing for the children. Tamara realized that many items in their goody bags were for older children. Some of the toys might even be unsafe for these

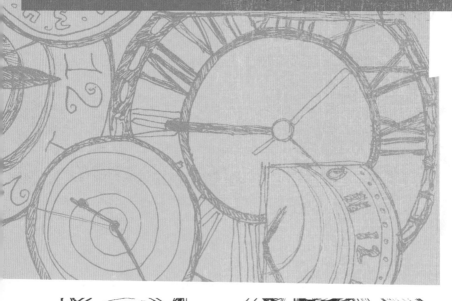

little kids. The social worker suggested that the girls give the bags to the local health clinic, where there never seemed to be anything for children to do. The girls agreed and headed off.

The clinic waiting room was packed. The harried receptionist, trying to attend to everyone, motioned for the girls to drop off the bags in a hallway behind her desk. When Tamara, Gayle, and Leticia got outside, they felt deflated. Tamara said she even felt "a little silly." She wondered out loud, "Which kids will get the goody bags?" Leticia responded, "Yeah, it's hard to know if we really did any good." Gayle summed up how they were all feeling: "Yep, maybe we should have made a list or chart or something to really think it through."

think about it, talk about it

- What motivated the girls to do something for the kids at the shelter?

- Were their actions organized to meet a genuine need or an imagined one? What's the difference?

- What planning steps did the team of girls skip over?

- What did they do well?

- Were their efforts a good use of their time and resources? Why or why not?

- Flip the script: If you and your friends had just read the same newspaper article and wanted to do something about domestic violence in your area, what are the first steps you might take?

2. The Case of the Boys in the Halls

Jennifer noticed a disturbing trend in the crowded halls of her high school: Boys very obviously eyeballed girls up and down and then mouthed off crude comments. Any adults in the hallways either didn't hear or pretended not to. Jennifer guessed they didn't think the remarks were as important as watching out for physical harm.

Jennifer started talking about the boys' crude behavior with a few of her friends. She asked: "Do you think there's a line between fun flirting and affection and some of this stuff we hear and see?" Isabelle agreed: "You know, I never really thought about it, but you're right. When boys do that, all the hallways feel like meat markets."

Isabelle and Jennifer decided to conduct a mini survey in the school cafeteria and library. They surveyed 30 girls and found:

- 25 of them felt humiliated by the boys' behavior.

- All 30 felt that adults should pay more attention to verbal abuse among students.

- 15 girls thought the situation warranted action.

Jennifer and Isabelle called a meeting and asked their two favorite teachers to be advisers. Twelve girls came. Together, the girls created this mini action plan, which they put into place over a few weeks:

- They visited the principal to discuss the problem and ask for help with solutions.

- With the principal's support, the girls decided to hold a few honest, small-group discussions with girls, boys, and adult advisers. During the talks, girls asked boys to think about how their actions affected girls, and together they worked out some agreements.

Meanwhile, the principal agreed to ask the school staff to pay more attention to verbal abuse in the hallways and to help kids understand the impact of their comments and gestures.

At the end of six weeks, Jennifer and Isabelle conducted a second survey. The results? Girls felt more comfortable at school and less worried about unwanted remarks in the hallways. The girls could have stopped there (they'd already done enough "taking action" to earn Visionary Awards!), but they were inspired and decided to keep at it.

They rallied a team to meet again (this time, some of the boys came). This new team wrote down all the steps they had taken, with some tips for implementing them. Then, with their principal's support, they visited other high schools in their state to try to spread the solutions they were creating.

think about it, talk about it

- How did Jennifer and Isabelle know that what mattered to them also mattered to other girls?

- How did the girls get support for their ideas?

- What resources did the team need to carry out their plan? Did their initial plan require a lot of supplies or money?

- What happened when they reached out and involved others?

- What impact did their actions have? What would make it more sustainable?

- What could they do to keep their snowball going, even if they personally didn't have time to keep building it?

Ideas for Taking Action

It's your turn! Go ahead, take action! Here are some ideas.

Think globally, act locally!

After seeing a documentary about how thousands of elephants are killed each year by poachers who want their ivory tusks, you might feel the desire to get out and do something about it. But you can't just hop on a plane to Africa. So what can you do?

You could educate others about the poaching, and perhaps even drum up support for a local boycott of ivory jewelry and other ivory goods. Or you could use the issue as a springboard to other animal-related causes. Perhaps you could take action to improve the treatment of animals in a local zoo or shelter or protect a local endangered animal.

The same applies to improving the world for girls. In 2005, an estimated 58 million girls around the world were still not in school, and of those who were, one in four weren't expected to complete fifth grade. Experts say that educating girls is one of the most beneficial commitments a country can make, because it not only prepares girls for higher education, it helps pull families out of poverty, hunger, and ill health. Here's what one American woman did while on a trip to Africa:

One Woman's Gift to Girls: Hope

While on vacation in Rwanda, Cheryl Baldwin, an executive director at Long Island University in Brookville, New York, saw how poverty and despair were affecting girls in a country still reeling from civil war. So she came up with a vision—Camp Hope, a leadership development program for Rwandan girls. In the summer of 2007, through Baldwin's efforts and funding from an anonymous donor, 20 Rwandan girls met with Rwandan senators and other women leaders to discuss girls' concerns. In 2008, the camp plans to serve 60 girls. One girl reported that Camp Hope gave her "the opportunity to hope again." "I was very desperate," she said. "I couldn't see anything good for me in the future. . . . I now know that I am precious and valued in the Rwandan society."

What can you do to help girls worldwide get an education? Start in your community! Remember: Raising local literacy levels raises world literacy, too.

indignation

\in-dig-NĀ-shən\ noun: the feeling of anger mingled with contempt or disgust, aroused by injustice

Have you ever felt a little righteous indignation? Maybe you feel it when you use your girl's-eye view of the world? Consider using a little RI to find your Take Action issue. Below are a few thoughts to get you going. And, remember: If these ideas don't spark your thinking, talk to friends, read the newspaper, surf the 'Net to find your own. It's easiest to act when you're inspired!

Love That Song?

What's your favorite music station? What songs are played the most? Make a list of lyrics that you think disrespect women or girls. Do you know any lyrics that disrespect men and boys? Is there a Take Action Project for you here? Maybe organizing a few friends to meet with someone at a local radio station to ask for a 30-minute (or even 15) timeslot for some tunes that lift girl spirits, and then writing a letter to your school or local newspaper about the results? Or maybe go bigger—organize lots of girls (you've got 2.6 million sisters in Girl Scouts) to make the same request at radio stations around the country: Slots for girl deejays, for a day, a year…forever?
And that's just radio stations. Then there are magazines, movies, TV shows!

Who Makes What?
Who Does What?

Yes, on average, men still make more money than women—and for some reason, men often end up in fields that tend to be higher paying. Why? Perhaps your Take Action Project could lead you to some answers—and improvements.

It's not that you'd want men to make less, but perhaps you, your girlfriends, your aunts, or cousins would like to add to your earning power—and that of women around the world. What's a Take Action Project for you here? How about inviting women who have been financially successful—in a career path that is unusual for women—to host a discussion at your high school or place of worship, or at a Girl Scout session? Try identifying women through your local newspaper or university, or even your network of adults. Kick the impact up a notch by spreading what you learn on to another group or asking your school to take the idea over as an annual event. Perhaps you want to research interesting careers in science, math, and technology (where there tend to be fewer women) and present the ideas you come up with to other girls in your area. Kick it up a notch and get companies in these fields to offer internships to girls.

These two Web sites might spark your thinking, too:

womankind.org.uk "This is not to say all men are rich, rather to recognize that whether men are rich or poor, women are almost always poorer."

catalyst.org, whose mission is creating inclusive environments and expanding opportunities for women in business.

What percent of the works in the world's museums are by women?

Invisible Artists?

Women earn the majority of degrees in the fine arts—bachelor's degrees all the way up to PhDs. Even so, an art degree isn't a ticket to art stardom. In fact, the art on view at galleries and museums is mostly by men. It has been estimated that for many years only 5 percent of the art on view in museums around the world was by women.

What are the galleries and museums in your area showing?

- Check out some shows and do the math.
- If women artists are underrepresented, consider writing a letter to the gallery owner or the museum's board of directors asking them to make a better effort to seek out works by women artists in future shows.

You can kick this up a notch by seeking out like-minded Girl Scout Seniors in Girl Scout councils around the country.

- Ask them to follow your lead and conduct their own surveys.
- If the results are the same, start making copies of your letter. Why not have it land on the desks of gallery owners and art museum boards around the nation?

You are about to flip to a 12-stage "Take Action" planning chart. It will guide you to use your brainpower to achieve the most impact you can, while using your time and resources wisely on one aspect of an issue you care about. So go ahead, bring the world one step closer to GIRLtopia! (And avoid the "case of the goody bags.")

Take Action Planning Chart
A LIFE-LONG TOOL FOR THINKING THROUGH ANY PROJECT

Take Action Stages You can use these for any Take Action Project.	Tips What would make life better for girls?	Tools These tools are included in this journey to help guide you.	Page	Log It! For Visionary Award, fill in your steps as they are completed.
1. What are the issues?	Brainstorm needs/issues/problems that concern you. Research!	• Surveys • Interviews • Brainstorm	86 89 82	
2. Which issue are you choosing?	What do you think really needs to change? Make a group decision if you're working with a team.	• Community mapping • Brainstorm	91 82	
3. What are possible solutions?	Brainstorm ideas for your Take Action Project.	• ID issue	82	
4. Which solution are you choosing?	Based on your time, resources, and desired impact, define your project and write your goal.	• Take Action statement	94	
5. How will you know when you've succeeded?	Create your goals and evaluation criteria. How will you measure success?	• Vision	14–16, 94	
6. Set up a time line or calendar.	What tasks need to be completed? By whom? By when?	• Time line	99	

Take Action Stages You can use these for any Take Action Project.	Tips What would make life better for girls?	Tools These tools are included in this journey to help guide you.	Page	Log It! For Visionary Award, fill in your steps as they are completed.
7. What resources will you need?	Info? Skills? Things? People power?	• Community mapping • Confidence	91 38	
8. Who can help?	Who in your community can you partner with? How can you network?	• Community mapping	91	
9. Who will do what?	Distribute tasks and responsibilities if you're working on a team.	• Teamwork	62	
10. Do!	Implement your action plan.	• Voice • Publicity • This chart!	34 96	
11. Evaluate!	Did you fulfill your goals?	• Evaluation	102	
12. Reflect and celebrate!	Thank your supporters and share your legacy.	• Appreciation • Reflection	100 104	

brain-storm

Identify an issue in your community

What action can you take to bring the world closer to your vision of GIRLtopia? Consider an idea from your art project or choose something new to take action on.

Use news stories, surveys, and interviews to find out what your community needs are.

Which issues are you most passionate about? Write them here.

....
....
....
....
....
....
....
....

Which of these issues do you want to focus on? Write them here.

....
....
....
....
....
....
....
....

- Which issue do you want to choose for your Take Action Project? Write it in the center circle below.

- What are possible solutions? Write them in the outer circles below.

Possible solution #1

Possible solution #2

My Take Action Project issue is:

Possible solution #3

Possible solution #4

research

\ri-SəRCH\ verb: to collect information about a particular subject

Knowledge is power. So, to make the most impact with your Take Action Project, you'll want to be fully informed about the issue you are addressing. Good leaders also think critically about the world. That's where research comes in.

EXISTING INFORMATION
(printed material, Web sites, other media)
(see next research page)

SURVEYS
(see survey page)

INTERVIEWS
(see interview page)

finding information

Here are some questions to guide your research on an issue:

- Who is affected? Directly? Indirectly? (age and/or ethnic group, community/neighborhood)
- How are people affected? (Are rights being violated? Is quality of life impacted? Do some people benefit from the situation? Who and how?)
- Why are people affected? (What is the underlying cause of the issue? What factors play a part in this issue? Is one group affected more than others? Why?)
- What solutions or actions have already been tried or suggested?
- What solution or action might be most effective?
- Who is in a position to bring about change?
- Who or what stands in the way of change?

Finding and Assessing Information

The world is filled with information, and much of it is readily available—especially on the Internet. The key is to find information that is reliable. Start with:

- Printed material in newspapers, books, magazines, and journals
- Web sites of nongovernmental organizations, schools and universities, governments, corporations, and local businesses
- Other media, including news broadcasts, documentaries, dramatizations, movies, and videos

As you research, keep in mind that not all information is created equal. In other words, not all information is reliable. Cross-check facts and conclusions, especially controversial ones. Consult multiple sources. To assess the reliability of a source, ask these questions:

- Who is financing or supporting this source?

- What are the qualifications of the writer(s)?

- Who is the information aimed at?

- Do the authors and sponsors have any interests/goals/beliefs that might influence the way they present information?

- Where did the authors get their facts? Do they cite sources? Are these sources reliable?

- Is the information up-to-date?

When doing research online, these questions are particularly important, because anyone

Be Wary of Statistics

Statistics often sound convincing, but their reliability must be verified. Check the reputation of the source. Look for a description of how and from whom the statistics were collected.

To shed light on a local issue, you may want to collect your own statistics. See "survey" on the next page.

85

survey

\SəR-vā'\ noun: a sampling or examination of facts, figures, or opinions

What do girls in your community think an ideal world would be? What are their concerns and needs? There's only one way to find out: ask! Surveys can provide firsthand information on how an issue affects your community, and they give you insight into what girls think. Surveys also allow you to identify potential supporters.

To CREATE a survey, identify the information you need and then develop a questionnaire that will collect it efficiently. Follow these tips:

- Keep your questionnaire short and simple.

- Each question should target only one issue and be as clear and specific as possible.

- Three basic types of questions are:
  1) rating questions (on a scale of 1–5, smiley and frown faces, strongly agree/disagree)
  2) yes/no/explain questions
  3) open-ended questions

- Set up your survey so people can easily mark their answers from multiple options; this also makes it easy to analyze the results. (See sample survey, page 88.)

- Include basic questions about the respondent (age group, school year); this will also help you analyze the results (see page 88).

- Avoid "leading questions" or questions that seem to invite a particular answer, such as "Do you think safety is important?"

- Do not collect any information that can identify the respondents. Let respondents know that their answers will remain anonymous.

Surveys can be conducted in person, or by phone, mail, or e-mail. For all methods, follow these tips:

- Always be polite. If someone does not want to participate, respect her wishes.

- Consult teachers and caregivers about safety. If collecting data in person, work in pairs.

- Explain what the survey is for: "A project by Girl Scouts in your area on ___."

- Do not express your own opinion about any of the questions.

To ANALYZE the data, follow these tips:

- Add the totals for each multiple-choice answer and organize them in a table.

- Work out what percentage each total represents (divide the total by the number of people who responded to the question and then multiply by 100).

- Write a summary report. Include the table. Highlight significant results. Draw conclusions. Include where and how you collected the information, who the respondents were (age, community), and how many took part. Include a copy of your survey in your report. Send your report to local media with a cover letter explaining the purpose of your survey (see "publicity" on page 96).

The Girl-Friendly Community Survey

Our group, Girl Scout Team No. 1234, is conducting a survey about what our community needs to make it more girl-friendly. Please take a few moments to answer the questions below. This information will help our campaign to make our community a safer and more empowering place for girls. All information will remain anonymous. Thank you for taking part in our survey.

Please circle the answers you choose clearly or clearly write in your own responses.

1.   What is your age?   under 10   10–13   14–16   17–19   over 19

2.   What community do you live in?   West Side   East Side   South Side   North Side

3.   Do you think your community is safe for girls?   Yes   No

4.   Which do you think would make your community safer for girls?
     More police   More streetlights   More after-school programs

     Other (please explain) _____

5.   Read this statement: Girls in my neighborhood would be really interested in more arts programs. Do you:
     a. strongly agree   c. disagree
     b. agree   d. strongly disagree

6.   [Your question here:] _____

7.   [Your question here:] _____

8.   If you could create one new program for girls in your community, what would it be?

     _____

9.   Would you be interested in supporting our campaign to get more arts programs for girls in your neighborhood?   Yes   No

Please return this survey to:
(Address)

interview

\in-tər-VYÜ\ noun: a meeting at which information is obtained

Interviews can provide deeper and more detailed information than a survey. Personal testimony gathered in an interview can also be a powerful force for change.

How to Conduct an Interview:

Determine your purpose. Ask yourself: How can I use personal testimony to accomplish my goals?

Do some research before the interview to establish your knowledge base (see research, pages 84–85).

Select interviewees. Ask yourself: Who has the information I need? Who will provide it?

Contact interviewees to determine their availability and any special needs.

In selecting a location, consider situational constraints (a noisy room makes interviewing difficult).

Prepare your questions in advance. Order them logically. Start with easy questions (the person's age, community). Group questions on the same topic. Use words the interviewee will understand. Be specific. Avoid words that might offend.

Test your questions on members of your group before conducting the interview.

On interview day, arrive on time and dress appropriately.

Explain your purpose, and make clear that the interview will be anonymous.

To record the interview, ask the person's permission. But don't rely on the recording. Take thorough notes. Use the recording only for clarification.

How to Get the Most Out of an Interview:

A good interviewer is skilled in listening and encouraging people to talk.
Here are some tips:

- Remain quiet and let the person talk; encourage the person: "I see; tell me more."

- Probe: — For depth of content: "Could you explain that process to me?"

  — To increase clarity: "Could you explain what you mean when you call the situation 'shameful'?"

  — For a reaction: "A recent editorial in a local newspaper called the situation 'under control.' Do you agree? Could you explain?"

- Keep the interview on track: "Let's return to what you said earlier about ___" or "Tell me more about ___."

- Ask summary questions: "If I understand you correctly, you are saying that ___."

- Fact check as you interview: "Is your sister 11 or 12?" "Did that happen this year or last year?"

- Ask hypothetical questions: "If you could change one thing in your community, what would it be?"

- End by asking: "Is there anything else you would like to add?" "Is there anything I didn't ask that you hoped I would?"

mapping

\MA-ping\ noun: a dynamic way of assessing a community's resources

Community mapping is a way of highlighting a community's assets—the people, things, services, organizations, and businesses that exist in a given area. A leader assesses community resources in order to: (1) identify community needs and (2) identify assets that might support her project.

Support from community assets can come in various forms:

- sponsors (people/organizations that allow you to use their name to lend authority to your project in order to gain additional support)

- information (data already collected on a local issue; access to archives)

- networking (relationships and connections to additional individuals, groups, organizations)

- materials (use of video cameras, computer access, printing)

- space (meeting/rehearsal space for events, press conferences)

- services (video editing, photocopying)

- skills (shooting/editing videotape, publicity)

- personnel (cameraperson, reporters, other)

- publicity (putting out the word about your project)

Be sure to get outside to map your community. As Juliette Gordon Low said, "Sun and air are life-giving."

To start your community mapping, answer the questions below. Then go to the community mapping chart on the next page.

- What nonprofit organizations in your area work on issues related to your project? (If you don't know, see "research," page 84.)

....
....

- What individuals have skills, knowledge, tools, or resources that you need?

....
....

- What businesses might be interested in sponsoring or supporting your project?

....
....

- If colleges or universities are in your area, which departments might you contact for support?

....
....

- What media outlets (newspapers, television and radio stations) are in your area?

....
....

- What faith organizations? Student organizations? Parent organizations? Senior citizens' groups?

....
....

- What civic organizations and government bodies might support your project?

....
....

Fill in the chart below to **map your community**'s assets and deficits.

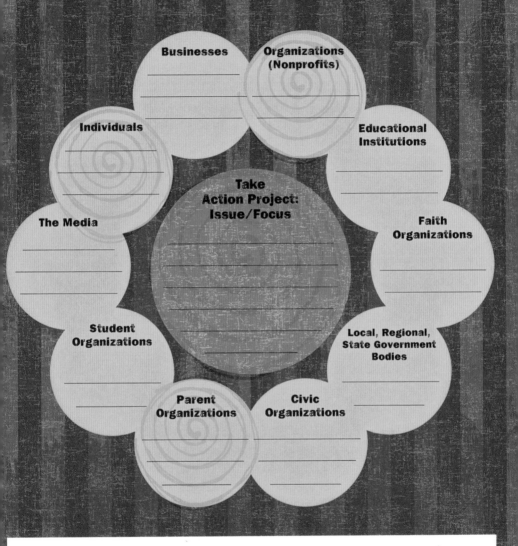

Businesses

Organizations (Nonprofits)

Individuals

Educational Institutions

Take Action Project: Issue/Focus

The Media

Faith Organizations

Student Organizations

Local, Regional, State Government Bodies

Parent Organizations

Civic Organizations

Did You Know? Women were pioneers in community mapping. In the 1890s, community activist Jane Addams decided to map community assets and deficits in Chicago's immigrant neighborhoods. She used this information to gain support for Hull House, a settlement house she founded to provide services and resources for newly arrived immigrants. Hull House became a national model of a one-stop community center offering everything from job training to a place for neighbors to gather.

Write Your Take Action Statement

Your statement:

- Expresses your vision for girls in your own words
- Explains the community issues you have identified and the plan of action you intend to take
- Motivates others to get involved

Use the sentence starters below to write your Take Action statement. Hold on to your statement—and your vision—as your project progresses. Use your statement as an evaluation tool when your project is complete.

My project focuses on these community issues:

....

My project involves this realistic plan of action:

....

My project goals are:

....

The impact of this project will be:

....

This project could be sustainable if:

....

I'll know I have succeeded because:

....

I found this inspirational quote to keep me motivated along the way:

....

public speaking

\pə-blik SPĒ-king\ noun: The act, art, or process of making effective speeches before an audience

Speaking up for what you believe in is an important leadership skill. Whether you want to address a town meeting, meet someone face-to-face, or give a presentation at school, these tips will guide you to become an effective advocate:

Be prepared. Know your subject. Jot down notes. Organize your points and be able to back them up (with personal anecdotes, statistics, current events).

Know your audience and make it clear how your project relates to them. Are you speaking to peers? Parents? Professionals? With peers, you might use slang, but not with professionals.

Practice. Ask friends or family to be your audience. Run through your speech several times. Get feedback and then try again. Make adjustments until you're comfortable and in control of your material. Practice as often as possible—even at the breakfast table.

Use body language effectively. Gesture to make a point, but avoid constant fiddling or shifting. If you can, videotape yourself and review the tape to refine your body language.

Stay relaxed. Easier said than done? Try this technique before speaking: Shake out your body and warm up your voice by dancing to, or singing, a favorite song.

Speak clearly. Don't rush. Look at your audience. Don't bury your face in your notes. If you make a mistake, just take a breath and keep going. It's OK to let your humanity show. After all, your audience is human, too.

Be confident. Stay focused on what your project means to you and how much you want others to support it.

Be a good listener. Train yourself to listen carefully to people's comments or questions.

Be enthusiastic! Let people feel your excitement. Positive energy is a magnet!

publicity

\pə-BLI-sə-tē\ noun: information disseminated through various media to attract public notice

Publicity is critical for increasing awareness about your cause. To conduct a successful publicity campaign, communicate the who, what, when, where, why, and how:

Posters:

Model your design on magazine or billboard campaigns you find effective. See if you can find a community resource (see mapping, page 91) to donate production or copying services. Get permission to hang your posters anywhere your target audience will see them (schools, shops, supermarkets, libraries).

Fliers/Fact Sheets

are a great way to get the word out. Use the back of fliers to list relevant facts—clearly and in bulleted form, with sources. (See "research," page 84.) Get permission to distribute your fliers in schools, shops, pools, supermarkets, libraries.

E-campaign:

Create an electronic flier with a catchy graphic or photo and fast facts about your project. Write a short, explanatory cover note ("Dear Friends and Family: This is a project I've been working on for several months . . ."). Ask those on your mailing list to post your flier or forward it to others. Write an eye-catching title in the Subject line (Girls Take Back the Streets: Join Us!). Before you hit the Send button, spell-check everything and verify all details (date, time, place).

60-second pitch:

Put together a short, pithy story that grabs the listener's attention and gets your point across. Include all the main facts, plus an interesting anecdote. Rehearse it until you can recite it enthusiastically at any time to anyone.

The Media:

To get the word out to TV, radio, newspapers/news sites, and magazines, write a news release (see sample release on page 98). Get the names of the most appropriate editors or reporters to receive your release. Check the deadlines (sometimes several weeks in advance) for listing local events on community calendars, and get your news release in on time. Reach out to college TV and radio stations, too.

Taking Action with Publicity

For her Girl Scout Gold Award project, Tamaron, 17, decided to help the Chinatown community of Oakland, California, by promoting hepatitis B awareness. Tamaron, who is fluent in Chinese and interested in medicine, created an informative brochure and passed out more than 400 copies. She also promoted free hepatitis B screenings at a local lab. About 150 people signed up—and they brought their families and friends to sign up, too. Tamaron calls it the "chain reaction of knowledge." And the chain continues: The brochure is still circulating in the community.

Sample News Release

When writing your news release, be sure to include the who, what, when, where, why, and how. And be sure all lines of the text are double-spaced.

FOR IMMEDIATE RELEASE
[date]

FOR MORE INFORMATION, CONTACT:
[name, phone, e-mail]

Girl Scouts Announce Findings of Community Safety Survey,

Present "We're All in This Together" Teen Safety Fair

Join your local Girl Scouts for a "We're All In This Together" Teen Safety Fair on Saturday, April 2, from 2 to 4 p.m. at the Tompkins Square Public Library on Tompkins Street and Maplewood Avenues. The fair will offer teens a variety of options for staying safe and having fun during after-school hours.

The fair tops off a three-month project about teen safety in the streets of our community that the [your group's name] group created and carried out. The girls will be presenting the findings from a study they conducted that shows teens are at risk on our streets before and after school hours. In particular, they found that many students face dangerous situations (peer confrontations) on their way to and from public transportation.

At the fair, teens will have an opportunity to sign up for a new service, started by this team of intrepid Girl Scouts, which pairs older students with younger ones to accompany them to and from drop-off points, before and after school. Many local organizations supported this effort, which led the girls to organize the "We're All In This Together" Teen Safety Fair.

Teens can also find out about a variety of organizations that offer exciting after-school programs. The [a local school or organization] will be giving demonstrations. Students from the [a local school or organization] will perform. Teens can sign up for these and other after-school programs and learn about scholarship opportunities. Also, Teen Health Yes!, a project of the local hospital, will offer free fitness counseling.

For their work in promoting teen safety in their community, the girls of [name here] have earned their Girl Scout Senior Visionary Awards. "These girls have shown the true qualities of Girl Scout leadership: courage, confidence, and character," says [your council name here] Girl Scout Council CEO [name here].

Please join the girls in their fight for teen safety on the streets of our communities at the "We're All In This Together" Teen Safety Fair.

CHANGE IT! Part 3 of the Visionary Award

Take Action Project Time Line

Task	Person Responsible	Date Needed

TAKE ACTION PROCESS
ACCOMPLISHED

_ _ _ _ _ _ _ _ _ _ _ _ _ _ _ _ _ _ _ _

Signature   Date

appreciation

\ə-prē-shē-Ā-shən\ noun: an expression of admiration, approval, or gratitude

{

Acknowledge Your Supporters

List the relevant information for everyone who supported you. Don't forget those who offered encouragement and moral support or provided snacks or advice. Use the list to send out your thank-you letters (see sample on the next page).

People Who Helped	What They Did	Address	Phone/Email

Girl Scout Troop No. 1234
4321 Southside Dr.
Anytown, VA 00000

Jennifer Lewis
Director, Women's Studies Program
Springfield Community College
6767 Winston St.
Springfield, VA 30045
(000) 000-0000

April 21, 2008

Dear Ms. Lewis:

I am writing to thank you for helping our Girl Scout Group No. 1234 complete our Take Action Project to make our city a safer place for girls. Thanks to you, we connected with some students at the Community College who worked with us to videotape our event. In addition, you pointed us to several other important resources, including the Girl Filmmakers Web site.

We are sorry that you were unable to attend our "Girls Take Back the Streets" event, but we are sending you a copy of our DVD for your viewing pleasure.

We appreciate your time and consideration on our behalf.

From all of us, thank you again,

Ayisha Thompson

Ayisha Thompson
Coordinator, Take-Action Outreach
GIRLtopia Team, Troop No. 1234

evaluation

\i-val-yə-WĀ-shən\ noun: the act of finding the value or worth of something

Evaluating a project lets you measure the impact of your efforts, learn from your experience, and celebrate your success. Use the following checklist and questions to evaluate your Take Action Project. If you were on your own for the entire project, consider the "we/our" as "I/my."

Checklist

1. Did we do the necessary research? [yes] [no]

2. Did we complete our project planning on time? [yes] [no]

3. Were we successful in getting community support? [yes] [no]

4. Did we anticipate all the problems we faced? [yes] [no]

5. Was our publicity campaign successful? [yes] [no]

6. How many people attended our event? ....

7. Did we stay within our budget? [yes] [no]

8. Did we fulfill our goals? [yes] [no]

9. Did all team members make significant contributions? [yes] [no]

10. Did we send thank-you letters to supporters? [yes] [no]

Follow-Up Questions

- What did we do well?

- What could we have done better?

- What obstacles did we face?

- What obstacles got in the way of fullfilling our responsibilities?

- How could we improve our trouble-shooting skills?

- How could we improve our publicity efforts?

- How could we get more people to attend?

- What was our budget?

- How much did we spend?

- Are there people we'd like to partner with in the future?

- What should we remember for next time?

- Did we make an impact?

- Will the impact be sustainable in some way?

- Is there anyone we still need to thank?

reflection

\ri-FLEK-shən\ noun: to express a thought or opinion resulting from contemplation

Take time out to contemplate your entire GIRLtopia experience—as a group and personally.

Check the statements that apply to your experience with the group:

_____ My effort made a difference to the whole group. **Yes/No**

_____ I enjoyed working together with the group. **Yes/No**

_____ I complimented or gave another girl positive feedback. **Yes/No**

_____ We all shared the same goal. **Yes/No**

_____ They couldn't have done it without me. **Yes/No**

Our experiences/activities:

_____ were fun

_____ were interesting

_____ were meaningful

_____ felt like school

_____ made sense to me

_____ can relate to my life

Circle one statement that describes your group experience:

- We couldn't have done it without one another.

- We tried to be only with people we like.

- It was every girl for herself.

Now reflect in your own words:

What skills and/or talents did you use and personally contribute to the project?

....

....

What was one of the most meaningful things you learned on this journey?

....

....

What qualities, skills, values, or talents did you acquire along the way?

....

....

If you could give yourself one piece of advice for becoming the "ideal" you, what would it be?

....

....

> ❝Vision without action is merely a dream. Action without vision just passes the time. Vision with action can change the world.❞
>
> — Joel Barker, futurist, filmmaker, and author, from "The Power of Vision"

ARE YOU A VISIONARY?

Take a look at your visionary list on page 17. Of the Top 10 qualities, skills, values, or talents you identified, which apply to your personal experience on this GIRLtopia journey?

celebrate

\SĔ-lə-brāt'\ verb: to praise widely, make known publicly, proclaim

Congratulations!
You've completed your journey!

You learned about **the state of the world for girls**, you discovered **YOUtopia**, you made connections along **the way to GIRLtopia**, and you worked to bring the world closer to **your ideal vision**.

How has this experience changed you?

If you had **one more wish** for expanding your GIRLtopia vision around the globe, what would it be?

Now, take time to celebrate. Gather your friends and family, and take a moment to share your accomplishments—and your vision of how much better the world can be—for all girls.

JOURNEY COMPLETED

Signature _____ Date